THE NUTRI NINJA MASTER PREP BLENDER SMOOTHIE BOOK

101 Superfood Smoothie Recipes For Energy,
Health and Weight Loss!

by Lisa Brian

Legal Disclaimer

Table of Contents

Legal Disclaimer

CHAPTERS:

Why You Need This Book

This Is The ONLY Smoothie Book Written Specifically For The Ninja Blender, Nutri Ninja, And Ninja Master.

There are other books out there that will tell you how to make smoothies, but this is the only book out there that will tell you how to make the BEST smoothies with your superior Ninja blender and how to get the most out of the ingredients you put into the Ninja to enrich your life.

As you'll see when you read a little further, Ninja blenders are different from other blenders because you're not simply juicing and discarding the pulp and other nutrients, the Ninja blender pulverizes and emulsifies fruits and vegetables to give you the highest possible amount of nutrients from each piece of vegetable and fruit you put into it.

This book is a must have and is an essential part of owning the Ninja Blender.

101 Of The Most Beneficial And Delicious Smoothie Recipes

This informative book gives you enough recipes to last for several months, having a different smoothie each day. Of course, if you mix and match and experiment with the recipes, then you could actually have a different smoothie each day for 365 days a year.

The recipes are designed specifically for your durable and long-lasting Ninja Blender, and they are kitchen tested for taste and categorized for your specific and general health needs.

Pro Nutritional Tips About Smoothie Ingredients

Become a smoothie expert! Besides getting healthier each day by using the Ninja Blender to make delicious meal replacement smoothies, the nutritional tips in this book will make you more as aware of what you're eating and the nutritional benefits of each smoothie you whip up. You'll also become something of an expert once you start learning about all the vital and essential nutrients that your smoothie have in them.

It's The ONLY Smoothie Book You'll Ever Need.

This book is a perfect companion to the Ninja Blender. It is so complete that you really won't ever need to buy another smoothie book as long as you own your Ninja, which could be a long, long time. It covers the nutritional aspects of your smoothies, along with all the "how to's" we could think of that you might ask about. This book should be kept in the kitchen because you'll probably use it on a daily basis.

Why a Ninja Blender?

The Leading Advantage Of A Ninja Blended Smoothie Is That All The Nutrients And Fibers Are Locked In.

The Ninja Blender makes sure nothing is wasted. When you blend fruits and vegetables in your Ninja, the fiber, as well as every single bit of produce you put in is reduced down to its smallest size until it is similar in consistency to water. That process unlocks all the nutrients and makes it easier and quicker for the body to absorb them. Traditional juicers and blenders simply cut up the greens and the fruit and give you only a small percentage of the juice that is actually within the fruit itself. They also leave a lot of the fiber in a solid state, which is then discarded by the unfortunate juicer owner.

Ninja Blenders Aid In The Battle To Lose Weight.

Anyone who has ever tasted a fruit smoothie knows that they experienced something extraordinary that day. They also know that they felt better almost immediately and had a bit more energy that day. Another strange thing that they most likely felt, was a feeling of fullness and that their hunger was satisfied for several hours after they savored that fabulous drink. Many of the Ninja smoothie recipes in this book have been designed for weight loss. They are meal replacers, which are ultra delicious and keep you full and energetic for hours at a time.

Making A Smoothie Is Faster Than Making A Meal, (And Often More Nutritious)

How long does a traditional breakfast of pancakes, eggs and sausage take to cook? Probably a lot longer than anyone in today's modern culture wants to admit. You have to make the pancake batter, heat the skillet, fry the eggs, fry the sausages and let's say it takes a half an hour – at least. How long for a delicious tasting, meal replacement, protein and nutrient packed smoothie? Throw the washed veggies and fruit into the Ninja, along with protein powder, honey, yogurt, soy milk and whatever you feel like putting in there and you have breakfast in under five minutes. Plus, you have made the very healthy decision to skip the greasy, fat-filled, high cholesterol conventional breakfast that will keep you operating as if you're in a fog for the next few hours.

Smoothies Can Help You Heal

Smoothies Provide More Energy.

We all are grateful when we get an extra spurt of energy. Coffee and other caffeinated drinks, along with sugary snacks give us these bursts, but they just don't last very long and the come down is difficult and always at the wrong time. Ninja smoothies, on the other hand, can give us a steady flow of natural energy that lasts for hours. Fruit and vegetables do that, you know. And when the fruits and veggies are broken down to their most absorbable size, as in a Ninja smoothie, then you're getting all the energy and nutrients that were meant for you.

Ninja smoothies provide healthful and reliable energy for athletes, students, homemakers, business people and everyone who simply needs more stamina.

Smoothies Add More Fiber To Your Diet.

By using the Ninja Blender, your smoothies will provide more fiber (roughage), to your diet. Fiber can help keep our digestion working properly, help us lose weight, reduce the risk of heart disease and colon cancer, along with lowering the dangers of diabetes and stroke. Making smoothies with the Ninja Blender will increase the intake of fiber to your diet and will begin to flush toxins from your body as well as give you a feeling of fullness, which means that you will naturally want to eat less and lose weight.

Smoothies Provide Antioxidants To Prevent Or Delay Cell Damage.

Antioxidants are simply chemicals in the body that block the negative activity of other chemicals known as free radicals.

Free radicals can cause damage to our cells, which which could lead to cancer. The body naturally produces free radicals. Ninja smoothie recipes contain a great deal of fruits and vegetables, which are high in antioxidants and can help in the fight against free radicals. There are plenty of them and just a few of them are: blueberries, blackberries, strawberries, apples, kale, carrots and beets.

Smoothies Enable You To Lose Weight.

A smoothie a day keeps the pounds away. We coined that phrase because it's true. When you replace a meal with a smoothie, you can't help but to lose weight. You're getting a healthy meal in a glass instead of a long sit-down meal full of sugar, salt and some refined, indigestible, who knows what, that will take a day or more to digest.

The meal replacement Ninja smoothie gives you what your body needs and gives it to it in a delicious and easily digestible manner that will help you lose the pounds fast.

Ninja Smoothies Are The Easy Way To Get Superfoods Into Your Body.

Superfoods are special foods in a category all by themselves. They are extremely high in nutrients and generally low in calories, which can improve people's mental and physical health. Many superfoods are in our Ninja smoothie recipes and some of them include, blueberries, kale, beets, sweet potatoes, Swiss chard, spinach, chia seeds and flax seeds, to name a few. Ninja smoothies make simple to get a lot of superfoods into our bodies all at once in a quick, delicious way.

How To Use Your Ninja Blender

The Ninja Blender And Its Capabilities

Ninja blenders are a must have in today's modern kitchen. They are incredibly valuable and necessary tools for helping you to make just about anything you can imagine. Soups are a breeze for the Ninja, as well as scrumptious ice cream, which can be prepared in just minutes.

Bread dough can be made quickly, and salad dressing takes less than 60 seconds.

Salsa, Hollandaise sauce, peanut butter and of course, fresh juice and exquisite smoothies, can all be made with the Ninja blender.

There's almost no end to what the Ninja can do.

Basic Operations

The Ninja is extremely easy to use. All you have to do to start enjoying your Ninja blender is place it on a level, clean and dry surface and plug it in. Add your chosen ingredients to the cup and tightly attach the Pro Extractor Blades unit on to the cup by screwing it on tightly. (That will guarantee a good seal).

Turn the cup upside down and align the cup tabs with the motor base. Rotate the cup clockwise until it locks in place and you hear a click. Push the power button on and select the Auto-IQ pre-set that's right for your mixture. When it's done, the Auto-IQ will stop on its own, and your smoothie, or whatever else you have chosen to make is ready to go.

Always remember to unplug your Ninja when you're not using it.

Auto IQ – Nutrient And Vitamin Extraction

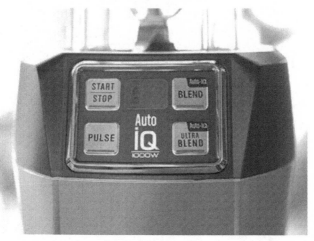

Auto-IQ is simply Ninja's one-touch intelligent controls. These control buttons on your Nutri Ninja have pre-programmed settings, which takes the guesswork out of drink and meal making.

These programs are designed and timed to deliver consistent, delicious results automatically, so all you have to do is push a button and enjoy!

The Auto-IQ has two settings. The first one is Auto-IQ BLEND.

This gives you consistent results in your drink and meal making by combining the pulsing and blending functions in your Nutri Ninja.

(Both the Auto-IQ settings use pauses in between the pulse and blend functions. This allows the ingredients to settle momentarily until the pulse or blend function kicks in again). When the timer reaches "0" (zero), the Ninja will stop by itself. This setting is used for fresh and softer ingredients to produce a smooth textured product.

The second setting is Auto-IQ ULTRA BLEND. This is used for harder, more fibrous ingredients, including frozen fruits and vegetables. It utilizes the pulse and blend functions, which gives you consistently smooth results.

Pro-Extractor Blades – The World's Most Powerful Nutrient And Vitamin Extraction Tool.

Ninja Pro Extractor blades are the most powerful blades out there because the proof is in the pudding, so to speak. It's also in the way that the blades break down all sorts of foods and ingredients, such as whole fruits and vegetables, ice, seeds and nuts and transform them into a smooth consistent texture.

The Ninja Pro Extractor blades speak for themselves and are unmatched in quality and results.

The Ninja Pro Extractor blades are able to convert a whole piece of fruit or vegetable into the smallest element, which is similar to the consistency of water. This means that ALL the nutrients are being utilized and nothing is wasted. Unlike other blenders and juicers, which produce a lot of waste and leave many of the nutrients and fiber out of the finished product,

Ninja's Pro Extractor blades break down everything that is put in front of them and leaves nothing for the garbage disposal. That way, you not only get your money's worth with the Ninja blender, but you also get your money's worth and all the nutrients that you paid for in the fruit and vegetables that you just bought.

Although the Nutri Ninja is multi-faceted and can make any number of foods, recipes and food combinations, we are focusing mainly on smoothies in this book. Just knowing the limitless possibilities of the Nutri Ninja is truly awesome in itself, and will no doubt come in handy at some point when you need to make some interesting dessert or exotic soup or salsa. Smoothies, however, are a lot of fun too, and they contain, in a drinkable version, all the nutrients that the human body craves, savors and needs to support general health and well being.

3 Speeds Target Different Food Types.

The Ninja Blender is so well engineered and precise that it lets you choose from three different speeds, including a pulse function, to perfectly blend, pulverize, crush or process foods. Each food type has unique properties, and each speed on the

Ninja blender is designed to accommodate those properties and give you the consistency that you desire. The speed settings, in conjunction with Ninja's well-constructed and highly durable blades, will give you the perfect smoothie and every time.

Speed Level 1

This speed is for processing and mixing. It enables you to produce exquisite fruit and vegetable purees to add to your smoothie.

Speed Level 2

Level 2 is for crushing and blending. This setting is the one you want to use when you need to grind nuts, crush ice cubes or blend heavily powdered smoothie beverages.

Speed Level 3

This is the setting that Ninja owners use for liquefying and pureeing. It's the perfect speed for mixing smoothies and liquefying thick mixtures. Whole fruits and vegetables will turn into impeccable smooth drinks retaining all of their nutrients when you use speed level 3.

Scrub No More

Clean up is a breeze with the Ninja. No more scrubbing and no more wondering if you really cleaned your blender thoroughly. The only caution is to be careful of Ninja's ultra-sharp blades. Never put your hand inside the pitcher because these blades are among the sharpest in the world. When you're done with the Ninja blender all you have to do is remove the lid and pop that, along with the pitcher and blade into the dishwasher.

The Ninja is dishwasher safe. Another method for cleaning your Ninja is:

Remove the Ninja blender lid and set it aside, then fill the Ninja pitcher up ¾ of the way with warm water.

Add just a drop of dishwashing detergent to the warm water and replace the Ninja lid snugly on to the top of the blender.

Press the Pulse button several times until your Ninja is thoroughly washed, then unplug the blender.

Rinse your Ninja in the sink until all the soap is gone and carefully remove the Ninja blade (following instructions in your manual).

To dry, simply place the Ninja blade, pitcher and lid on a towel.

Your Ninja blender is now sparkling clean and ready to use again.

Pro Tips for Making Amazing Smoothies

What To Add First?

Liquid – For an even texture and consistency of your smoothie, you should add half the amount of the liquid first and half at the end.

Protein powder – Add this ingredient next, right after the first liquid is poured into the blender. Powders thicken your smoothie and can give it a creamy texture.

When you add it early on, the powder will blend a lot easier and won't end up with a chalky quality to it.

Nuts, berries, flax seeds, sweeteners and peanut or almond butters – These blend in very well with the rest of the smoothie ingredients when they are in the middle of the blender mixture.

Leafy greens – If you add these at the beginning or at the end they may oxidize and lose some of their nutrients. They will also not be pulverized completely and there will be chunks of the leaves left in the smoothie.

Frozen fruit – Adding them at this level of the mix keeps the greens cool and enables the frozen fruit to blend much more efficiently.

Ice – Always add ice last. This will keep your greens and other foods from over heating and give your smoothie a cool and thick composition.

Liquid – After blending for a few moments, add the rest of the liquid and finish blending. This will give you the best quality blend you can get in a smoothie.

Fresh Or Frozen Fruit?

Fresh is always the best as far as optimal nutrition goes. Plus, the taste is extraordinary compared to frozen. The benefits of frozen, however, are still incredible. The old saying about the levels of nutrition is: fresh is best, then frozen, then canned. Frozen fruit in a smoothie is a tradition that will never die and there's no need for it to go away. Frozen fruit keeps your smoothie cool and makes it thicker.

Extracting Hidden Nutrition From Whole Fruits And Vegetables.

One of the truly nice things about the Nutri Ninja is that it utilizes the whole fruit and vegetable. It doesn't leave a pile of fibrous waste, which includes valuable nutrients, for you to simply toss away into your trashcan. The Nutri Ninja was purposely designed to extract ALL of the nutrients in each piece of fruit and vegetable you use. Other juicers and blenders were constructed to break down only the least difficult parts of the vegetables and fruit. They just don't have the strength and extracting power of the Nutri Ninja, which is capable of completely breaking down ingredients and extracting every possible hidden nutrient that they contain.

Prepare Portions Ahead Of Time.

If you love smoothies, like everybody else does, then you might as well prepare some of your ingredients ahead of time. That way, when you feel like having a smoothie, most of the work is already done. You can slice bananas, strawberries and any other fruit you may want and put them in a freezer bag and just pop them into the freezer.

Prep time will be cut in half (or more) and you can have a delicious smoothie in just a minute or two. Freezing carrots or beets or other hard vegetables, along with lettuce or dandelion greens is not recommended. They might end up to hard and could damage the blender.

Thickening Trick

If you add too much liquid to your smoothie, try adding a bit yogurt, oatmeal, avocado, banana or even chia seeds to thicken it up.

How To Store Your Smoothies

Storing Smoothies For Later

Make a double batch so you'll have a smoothie for later! Just store your extra smoothie in a glass container (Mason Jars are very good for this), with an airtight lid to keep it fresh. Fill it to the very top just to make sure no air gets inside. Professional smoothie makers always add a few drops of lemon juice to their smoothie and that extra vitamin C keeps it from oxidizing.

How To Use This Book

This book was written to make it easy for you to get the most out of your Ninja Blender. We've developed over a hundred delicious recipes that are exclusive to the Ninja Blenders and their owners. We've grouped these recipes into easy to find and even easier to read categories that focus on maintaining general vitality and targeting specific health concerns.

Smoothies For Health Conditions

These smoothie recipes deal with specific topics that many people are interested in.

These smoothies all have unique ingredients that focus on the targeted ailment and have shown to produce the desired results. The smoothies and their ingredients are not cures, and we are not claiming such. The ingredients used in these particular smoothies have worked for thousands of people and when taken in smoothie form, are easily digestible and quite delicious.

Some of the recipes deal with the following:

- Anti-Aging Smoothies
- Bone and Joints Smoothies
- Constipation Smoothies
- Detox Smoothies
- Blood Sugar Smoothies
- Immune System Smoothies

Lifestyle Smoothies

This smoothie section of the book has recipes that can actually enhance very definitive targets in one's life and health. The ingredients have been used by millions of people all around the world for generations and have pointed to the fact that certain foods, especially if it is readily digestible, (such as in smoothies), can have a highly beneficial outcome on the human body.

Some of the recipes in this section include:

- Beauty Smoothies
- Energy Smoothies
- Health Smoothies
- Heart Smoothies
- Kid Smoothies
- Mood Smoothies
- Performance Smoothies
- Stress Smoothies
- Weight Loss Smoothies

Recipes

Anti-Ultra Violet

Now you can help fight the negative effects of the sun on your skin from the inside out. This doesn't replace sunscreen, but it will help protect your sensitive skin from the sun's quite harmful ultra violet rays.

Servings: 2

calories: 205 | sodium: 319 mg | dietary fiber: 10.8 | total fat: 3.4 g | total carbs: 40.5 g | protein: 5.6 g

Ingredients

2 ½ cups coconut water
1 ½ oranges (sliced, peeled and seeds removed)
2 kiwis (peeled and sliced)
2 tbsp flaxseeds (preferably ground or in powder form)

Directions

1. Enjoy this wonderful tasting and practical drink after blending it at high speed for at least 45 seconds.

Berry Nice Indeed

This is jam packed with antioxidants! Combined with the vitamin C and E from the blueberries and strawberries, the Omega-3 from the flaxseeds make this a great anti-aging formula that will fight wrinkles and help your skin to glow.

Servings: 2

calories: 157 | sodium: 8 mg | dietary fiber: 6.0 | total fat: 10.8 g | total carbs: 15.6 g | protein: 2.0 g

Ingredients

½ cup strawberries

¾ cup blueberries

½ avocado

2 tsp ground flaxseed

1 cup ice cubes

Directions

1. Blend thoroughly for 30 – 45 seconds or until texture is smooth.

Green Is Keen

This rather simple drink can do wonders for your skin and health in general. There is a great deal of natural vitamin E and C in these ingredients, which are highly beneficial to your skin and to your over all beauty.

Servings: 2

calories: 835 | sodium: 71 mg | dietary fiber: 12.7 g | total fat: 77.2 g | total carbs: 44.0 g | protein: 9.7 g

Ingredients

1 ½ bananas

1 ½ cup spinach (chopped)

¼ cup avocado (peeled and pit removed)

2 tbsp sunflower seeds

¼ cup lemon juice (no seeds)

2 ½ cups soy or almond milk (low fat dairy milk is okay too)

3 tbsp sweetener (your choice)

Directions

1. Enjoy this great tasting smoothie
   after you blend it at high speed for
   approximately 45 seconds or until
   smooth.

Green Tea Coconut Strawberry

The ingredients in this smoothie will help keep your weight down and enhance your digestion, along with giving a youthful glow to your skin.

Servings: 2

calories: 464 | sodium: 276 mg | dietary fiber: 26.0 g | total fat: 17.2 g | total carbs: 67.0 g | protein: 15.3 g

Ingredients

2 tbsp green tea powder

1 ½ bananas

3 cups strawberries

2 cups coconut water

3 tbsp chia seeds

¼ cup plain yogurt

2 tbsp sweetener (honey or your choice).

Directions

1. Mix thoroughly in blender until texture is creamy smooth.

Kale Delight

Plenty of zinc and A and C vitamins here, along with calcium and other necessary minerals to keep your blood strong and youthful and infections and colds away.

Servings: 2

calories: 195 | sodium: 76 mg | dietary fiber: 4.0 | total fat: 2.9 g | total carbs: 40.0 g | protein: 6.5 g

Ingredients

1 banana

1 cup kale leaves (or collard greens or bok choy)

¼ cup pitted dates

1 cup arugula

1 cup milk (soy or almond milk is ok)

Directions

1. Blend for 30-45 seconds or until smooth.

Kale Is Queen

Kale is the queen of the super foods as far as some people would have it. It's packed with vitamins and minerals and is considered by many to be one of the best antioxidants in the world. It's great for detox and lowering cholesterol and it's super for your digestive and urinary systems.

Servings: 2

calories: 193 | sodium: 393 mg | dietary fiber: 9.2 g | total fat: 1.1 g | total carbs: 43.6 g | protein: 5.3g

Ingredients

2 carrots (cleaned and chopped)
2 cups kale (leaves only, no stems)
2 ½ cups coconut water
1 ½ apples (green preferably)
¼ cup lemon juice

Directions

1. You can enjoy this splendid libation after thoroughly blending at high speed for just under 1 minute.

Minty Coconut Blueberry

This smoothie even sounds like it tastes good. And it does! It also supplies your body with a great deal of vitamin C to help maintain your health and young looking self. The chia seeds will keep you feeling full for hours so you might even lose some weight if you keep this up.

Servings: 2

calories: 417 | sodium: 323 mg | dietary fiber: 19.6 g | total fat: 16.5 g | total carbs: 60.0 g | protein: 11.1 g

Ingredients

2 ½ cups coconut water
1 ½ cups blueberries
1 ½ cups strawberries
2 tsp chia seeds
¼ cup leaves of mint
2 tbsp lemon juice

Directions

1. Put ingredients in blender and blend at high speed for 45 seconds.

Peachy Blueberry

This smoothie is not only sweet and delicious, but it's loaded with plenty of vitamin C and E, among other things, which promotes youthful looking skin and hair, not to mention the benefits to your overall health.

Servings: 2

calories: 408 | sodium: 276 mg | dietary fiber: 19.1 g | total fat: 10.3 g | total carbs: 70.3 g | protein: 11.4 g

Ingredients

> 2 cups low fat milk or almond or soy milk
> 2 cups sliced peaches (fresh is best, then frozen, then canned)
> 1 cup blueberries

Directions

> 1. Add sweetener if desired, but it's usually not needed with this smoothie.

2. Blend everything for at high speed for at least 30 seconds or until texture is creamy smooth.

Pineapple Express

Pineapples, mangos, kale and coconut water all have wonderful nutrients to contribute to a more youthful and healthy appearance. Your newly moisturized and hydrated skin will probably be the first thing you'll notice if you start mixing these smoothies on a regular basis.

Servings: 2

calories: 408 | sodium: 276 mg | dietary fiber: 19.1 g | total fat: 10.3 g | total carbs: 70.3 g | protein: 11.4 g

Ingredients

2 cups pineapple chunks

1 ½ cup mango chunks

2 cups coconut water

1 ½ cups kale (chopped)

2 tbsp chia seeds

Directions

1. Blend this mixture for at least 35 seconds at high speed.

Pineapple Mango

This incredibly simple drink with only a few basic ingredients has the potential of transforming your health and your skin into how you've always envisioned yourself to be: glowingly young. Plenty of vitamins, minerals and Omega-3 in this one.

Servings: 2

calories: 341 | sodium: 317 mg | dietary fiber: 17.4 g | total fat: 10.3 g | total carbs: 53.9 g | protein: 9.8 g

Ingredients

1 ½ cups pineapple chunks
1 cup mango chunks
2 ½ cups coconut water
2 tbsp chia seeds

Directions

1. You can enjoy this right after you blend the ingredients at high speed for about 50 seconds.

Pure Gold

This is full of antioxidants and will keep you looking and feeling young. The ginger, with its immune boosting and cleansing effects will help you get the unwanted toxins out of your body.

Servings: 2

calories: 123 | sodium: 19 mg | dietary fiber: 4.0 | total fat: 0.4 g | total carbs: 30.5 g | protein: 1.5 g

Ingredients

½ carrot (sliced)

½ papaya (sliced)

1 orange (sliced)

½ cup pear juice

1 tsp sliced ginger

½ cup ice cubes

Directions

1. Blend 30 – 45 seconds or until smooth.

Relaxing

This recipe won't put you to sleep, but it will help relieve some of the day's stress. The minerals and other nutrients in this smoothie will work on your muscles, skin and mind to give you a relaxing, more confident feeling to face the world with.

Servings: 2

calories: 924 | sodium: 636 mg | dietary fiber: 26.4 | total fat: 41.4 g | total carbs: 119.6 g | protein: 0g

Ingredients

¾ cup dried oatmeal

¾ cup raw almonds (chopped finely)

1 ½ bananas

2 ½ cups coconut water.

2 -3 tbsp sweetener (your choice, though honey is preferred)

Directions

1. Get ready to relax after you blend at high speed for at least 45 seconds.

Wake Up

This high energy-producing smoothie also can fight those dark circles under your eyes. There are ample sources of vitamin C, A and Omega 3s in this potent potable.

Servings: 2

calories: 427 | sodium: 72 mg | dietary fiber: 17.1 g | total fat: 8.0 g | total carbs: 79.3 g | protein: 11.2 g

Ingredients

- 2 tbsp Goji berries
- 2 cups raspberries
- 2 cups blueberries
- 3 tbsp flaxseed powder (or ground flaxseed)
- 6 oz. plain or vanilla yogurt (low fat)
- 2 cups purified water or juice

Directions

1. Once in the blender, turn to high speed for 45 seconds or until thoroughly liquefied.

Wrinkle, Wrinkle. Go Away

Another not very complex recipe but extremely powerful in its beneficial effects on your overall health and particularly your skin. These simple ingredients tend to give your skin the nutrients it needs to become tighter and younger looking.

Servings: 2

calories: 547 | sodium: 328 mg | dietary fiber: 18.8 g | total fat: 32.5 g | total carbs: 64.3 g | protein: 7.5 g

Ingredients

2 cup blueberries

2 medium avocados (peeled and pitted)

2 tbsp flaxseed (ground if possible)

2 ½ cups coconut water

2 tbsp honey (or your choice of sweetener)

Directions

1. Savor this fantastic drink after blending at high speed for at least 40 seconds.

Osteo Punch

Your bones have never had it so good! Drink these on a regular basis and you'll not only feel stronger, but your bones and joints will probably be stronger.

Servings: 2

calories: 591 | sodium: 52 mg | dietary fiber: 12.3 | total fat: 56.1 g | total carbs: 25.3 g | protein: 9.1 g

Ingredients

½ avocado

½ cup broccoli

4 tbsp wheat bran

10 almonds

1 cup kale or spinach

1 ½ cups spring water or almond milk

Directions

1. Blend 30 – 45 seconds or until smooth.

Strong Bones

This smoothie will give you a mineral jolt, especially loaded with calcium and antioxidants, which support bone and joint strength.

Servings: 2

calories: 467 | sodium: 26 mg | dietary fiber: 10.6 | total fat: 31.8 g | total carbs: 42.2 g |protein: 13.1 g

Ingredients

½ banana
1 cup kale or romaine lettuce
½ cup blueberries
4 tbsp wheat bran
15 cashews
1 ½ cups spring water or any type of milk

Directions

1. Blend 30 – 45 seconds or until smooth.

Epsom Salt Surprise

This one will get your system working and in a relatively short amount of time. The Epsom salts pull water into the colon, which in turn makes it much easier to go to the restroom. After this smoothie you should sort of hang around the house for a while. Good luck!

Servings: 2

calories: 398 | sodium: 3,537 mg | dietary fiber: 10.4 | total fat: 1.4 g | total carbs: 98.4 g | protein: 6.7 g

Ingredients

½ cup applesauce
½ cup plain yogurt
1 tbsp Epsom salt
½ cup spring water
½ banana
½ cup ice cubes
5 pitted prunes

Directions

1. Blend until smooth, usually 30 – 45 seconds.

Prune

This smoothie is designed to relieve constipation. Prunes and apples have high fiber content and they're quite flavorful too.

Servings: 2

calories: 512 | sodium: 96 mg | dietary fiber: 9.1 | total fat: 2.1 g | total carbs: 120.9 g | protein: 9.9 g

Ingredients

5 pitted prunes
1 cup ice cubes
1 cup plain yogurt
½ tsp cinnamon powder
1 cup apple juice
2 tbsp honey (if desired for sweetness)

Directions

1. Blend until smooth.

Algae For Everyone

This smoothie contains so many beneficial elements in it that there just isn't room to mention them all. However, the blue-green algae, that we've added to this highly nutritious drink, is full of essential amino acids and has lot of protein.

Servings: 2

calories: 256 | sodium: 391 mg | dietary fiber: 10.5 g | total fat: 1.1 g | total carbs: 51.6 g | protein: 13.4 g

Ingredients

4 kale leaves (chopped)
½ cup spinach (chopped)
2 ½ cups coconut water
½ cup parsley leaves (no stems)
½ cup cilantro
2 apples (green preferably)
½ ginger root (grated)
2 tbsp blue-green algae powder

Directions

1. Blend thoroughly for about 55 seconds.

Avo-Cucumber

This one seems to have a bit of everything in it. Try it, you'll love it.

Servings: 2

calories: 236 | sodium: 189 mg | dietary fiber: 6.6 g | total fat: 10.9 g | total carbs: 23.8 g | protein: 14.1 g

Ingredients

½ avocado

½ cucumber

½ pear

¼ lemon

¼ cup cilantro

¾ inch ginger (sliced)

1 ½ cup kale (tightly packed)

¾ cup coconut water

¼ cup protein powder

2 cups water

Directions

1. Blend at high speed for 45 seconds or until smooth.

Beet This

This is almost the perfect detox recipe. It has a lot of nutrients that will benefit your whole body and beets to target your liver. It also fills you up for hours at a time.

Servings: 2

calories: 326 | sodium: 71 mg | dietary fiber: 17.2 g | total fat: 10.1 g | total carbs: 52.5 g | protein: 9.8 g

Ingredients

1 medium sized beet (cleaned and sliced)

2 apples (peeled, sliced and seeds and core removed)

1/3 cup parsley

2 tbsp chia seeds

¾ inch of ginger

1 ½ lemons (peeled, sliced and seeds removed)

2 cups kale leaves (chopped)

16 oz. purified water

Directions

1. Blend these ingredients for 1 minute at high speed or until the

2. Consistency is smooth with no chunks.

Berry Minty App

This tasty concoction will kee
works to gently detoxify your :

Servings: 2

calories: 93 | sodium: 18 mg | dietary fiber: 7.3 g |
total fat: 0.7 g | total carbs: 21.8 g | protein: 2.4 g

Ingredients

½ cup mixed berries (frozen or fresh)

10 leaves of mint

1 apple (peeled, sliced and seeds removed)

5 Romaine lettuce leaves

20 oz. purified water (use juice if desired)

Directions

1. Blend together for 45 seconds or until texture is just right for you.

Blue Ginger

This delicious, low calorie smoothie is jam-packed with antioxidants, vitamins and minerals and a super infection fighter and anti-inflammatory, commonly called ginger.

Servings: 2

calories: 366 | sodium: 179 mg | dietary fiber: 8.5 g | total fat: 7.2 g | total carbs: 66.7 g | protein: 13.6 g

Ingredients

½ cup blueberries
2 bananas (fresh or frozen
4 ice cubes
½ cup ginger juice
2 ½ cups soy milk (almond milk or low calorie milk is fine)

Directions

1. Put all ingredients into blender and blend at high speed for 45 seconds or until liquefied to taste.

Cilantro Detox

Cilantro is a very powerful detox element because it bonds with heavy metals in the body and helps in the elimination of these and other toxins. Cilantro also helps in lowering LDL or bad cholesterol levels and therefore benefits the heart function while it detoxes the body.

Servings: 2

calories: 334 | sodium: 98 mg | dietary fiber: 6.1 | total fat: 12.8 g | total carbs: 24.6 g | protein: 33.4g

Ingredients

½ avocado (sliced)

¼ lemon (peeled and de-seeded)

½ pear

¼ cucumber (peeled and sliced)

1 cup kale (or romaine lettuce)

½ oz. sliced ginger

3 oz. protein powder (hemp or pea)

3 tbsp cilantro (chopped)

Directions

1. Blend for 30 -45 seconds or until smooth.

Cranberry, Cranberry

Cranberries are terrific for detoxing the kidneys and they taste so good. Studies have also shown that cranberries can effectively fight urinary tract infections in men and women.

Servings: 2

calories: 247 | sodium: 21 mg | dietary fiber: 15.2 g | total fat: 0.0 g | total carbs: 64.6 g | protein: 2.7g

Ingredients

2 cups purified water or cranberry juice
¾ cup cranberries
1 cucumber (peeled)
1 celery stalk (sliced)
1 ½ apples (peeled, cored and seeds removed)
1 ½ pears (cored)
½ cup spinach

Directions

1. Blend together at high speed until consistency is smooth with no

2. chunks. (usually less than one minute).

Cucumber Kale

Cilantro is a great and natural detoxifier. Spinach and kale, besides being super nutritious, are cleansers as well. Toxins bind to these greens and are more easily eliminated from the body.

Servings: 2

calories: 39 | sodium: 20 mg | dietary fiber: 2.0 | total fat: 0.2 g | total carbs: 10.0 g | protein: 1.9 g

Ingredients

½ cucumber (sliced)
1 cup kale (or romaine lettuce or spinach)
1 ½ cups spring water
1/3 cup cilantro (chopped)
½ lemon (peeled and de-seeded)
1 wedge lime (peeled and de-seeded)
½ cup cilantro

Directions

1. Blend for 30 -45 seconds or until smooth.

Detox Berry

;reat while it cleans the toxins out of
/.

Servings: 2

calories: 321 | sodium: 49 mg | dietary fiber: 7.5 g
| total fat: 2.4 g | total carbs: 76.1 g | protein: 2.5 g

Ingredients

2/3 cup frozen cherries (pitted)
1 cup frozen raspberries
1 cup rice milk or almond milk
2 ½ tbsp. honey
1 ½ tbsp. ginger (finely grated)
2 tsp flaxseeds
1 tbsp lemon juice

Directions

1. Blend 45 seconds at high speed or
   until smooth.

Feel Good

This drink is loaded with antioxidants and has plenty of vitamins and energy giving nutrients. The Goji berry is also a noted stress reliever and has been shown to enhance your feeling of wellbeing.

Servings: 2

calories: 659 | sodium: 61 mg | dietary fiber: 17.4 g | total fat: 46.6 g | total carbs: 64.0 g | protein: 9.5 g

Ingredients

1 ½ cup blueberries

1 ½ cups coconut milk

¾ cup blackberries

¾ cup raspberries

¼ cup Goji berries (These should soak for 10-15 minutes before blending)

2 tbsp flaxseed (ground)

5 dates (pitted)

2 cups purified water

Directions

1. Blend all ingredients at high speed for at least 50 seconds or until liquefied.

Fiberlicious

Plenty of fiber in this one; it will keep you full and help you with regularity.

Servings: 2

calories: 849 | sodium: 189 mg | dietary fiber: 17.2 g | total fat: 72.9 g | total carbs: 39.3 g | protein: 21.2 g

Ingredients

2 cups almond milk or soymilk

½ avocado

1 pear (sliced)

1 ½ cups spinach (tightly packed)

½ cup coconut water

1 tbsp chia seeds

½ cup protein powder

2 ½ cups water

Directions

1. Blend until smooth – usually around 45 seconds.

Goji Goodness

This delightful libation will not only tickle your taste palate but it will help rid toxins from your system as it gives you a sense of wellbeing.

Servings: 2

calories: 214 | sodium: 361 mg | dietary fiber: 8.5 g | total fat: 1.6 g | total carbs: 50.9 g | protein: 5.1g

Ingredients

2 bananas
½ cup strawberries (frozen or fresh)
½ cup Goji berries
2 ½ cups coconut water
4 ice cubes

Directions

1. Blend these ingredients at high speed until the texture is silky smooth.

Jicama Surprise

The surprise is that it tastes so good. And it also provides plenty of vitamin C and fiber.

Servings: 2

calories: 407 | sodium: 85 mg | dietary fiber: 14.8 g | total fat: 21.0 g | total carbs: 48.5 g | protein: 14.6 g

Ingredients

1 lime
1 cucumber
1 apple
10 Romaine leaves
1 avocado
1 cup jicama (grated or sliced)
½ cup cilantro
½ cup protein powder
3 pitted dates
2 ½ cups water

Directions

1. Blend ingredients for 45 seconds at high speed or until texture is smooth.

Kale/Mango Detox

This is one of the easier detox smoothie to make. Besides being uniquely delicious, the ingredients make this smoothie high in fiber, iron, antioxidants, vitamins A, C, K and Calcium.

Servings: 2

calories: 151 | sodium: 43 mg | dietary fiber: 2.7 g | total fat: 0.5 g | total carbs: 35.2 g | protein: 3.6 g

Ingredients

1 ½ cups orange juice
¼ cup chopped parsley
1 ½ chopped celery stems
1 ½ cups cubed mango
1 ½ cups chopped kale leaves

Directions

1. Blend for 45 seconds or until texture is smooth.

Smooth As Silk

This recipe works on the inside and outside. It aids in alleviating toxins while it works to clarify and moisturize your complexion.

Servings: 2

calories: 420 | sodium: 161 mg | dietary fiber: 8.2 g | total fat: 14.6 g | total carbs: 77.0 g | protein: 3.2 g

Ingredients

2 apples (peeled, cored and seeds removed)

1 ½ limes (peeled, sliced and seeds removed)

¾ cup parsley (leaves only, no stems)

2 tbsp coconut oil

3 tbsp leaves of mint

1 large cucumber (peeled)

1 cup coconut water

2 cups purified water or juice

Directions

1. Blend all together for 50 seconds or until the texture is smooth as silk.

Spicy Carrot

This smoothie will straighten your hair and open your eyes. For sure, depending, of course, on how much jalapeno you add to it. Either way, this super drink is designed to maintain a healthy heart.

Servings: 2

calories: 141 | sodium: 410 mg | dietary fiber: 8.6 g | total fat: 0.7 g | total carbs: 30.8 g | protein: 4.4g

Ingredients

2-3 tomatoes
5 carrots
2 bell peppers (preferably red – sliced and seeds removed)
3 garlic cloves
3 celery stalks
1 cup spinach
1 red jalapeno (seeds removed)
½ cup water cress

Directions

1. After thoroughly washing and preparing ingredients, blend at

2. High speed for 45 seconds or until liquefied to a smooth texture.

Spirulina Special Source

The Aztecs used to carry spirulina with them when they went on long trips. It not only gave them nourishment but it helped them detox.

Servings: 2

calories: 542 | sodium: 126 mg | dietary fiber: 9.4 g | total fat: 39.9 g | total carbs: 38.6 g | protein: 17.2 g

Ingredients

1 banana

½ avocado

1 cup almond milk or soymilk

1 cup blueberries

1 tbsp spirulina powder

½ cup protein powder

2 cups water

Directions

1. Blend for 45 seconds or until smooth.

Super Cleanse

Parsley and celery are diuretics and help the body get rid of toxins. Kale and mangos enhance detoxification because of their superfood nutrients.

Servings: 2

calories: 149 | sodium: 29 mg | dietary fiber: 3.0 | total fat: 0.6 g | total carbs: 34.7 g | protein: 2.7 g

Ingredients

1 cup kale (or romaine lettuce)
1 cup orange juice
½ cup mango (sliced)
¼ cup parsley (chopped)
1 stalk celery (chopped)

Directions

1. Blend until smooth – usually 30 – 45 seconds.

Sweet Fruit Detox Special

This is sweet and powerful. You'll love the taste and you'll love what it does for you.

Servings: 2

calories: 364 | sodium: 245 mg | dietary fiber: 10.8 g | total fat: 7.2 g | total carbs: 64.4 g | protein: 16.2 g

Ingredients

1 ½ tbsp. lemon zest
2 ½ cups strawberries (fresh or frozen)
3 ½ cups non-dairy milk (your choice)
1 orange (peeled)
1 ½ bananas
2 cups spinach

Directions

1. Blend for 45 seconds at high speed or until texture is smooth.

Tangy Blueberry

This simple smoothly contains an extraordinary amount of B vitamins, along with vitamin C, K, E, and minerals such as iron, calcium, manganese and copper. It also helps in the fight against infections because of its antioxidant properties.

Servings: 2

calories: 38 | sodium: 1 mg | dietary fiber: 3.7 g | total fat: 0.0 g | total carbs: 13.0 g | protein: 0.9 g

Ingredients

½ cup blueberries

2 lemons (peeled, sliced and seeds removed)

2 tbsp sweetener (honey, or your choice)

2 ½ cups purified water

Directions

1. Blend these ingredients together for about 45 seconds or until the texture is right for you.

Zesty Apple

This smoothie is perfect for softening pain and inflammation, while it quietly works on detoxing your system.

Servings: 2

calories: 188 | sodium: 18 mg | dietary fiber: 7.6 g | total fat: 0.7 g | total carbs: 48.1 g | protein: 2.8 g

Ingredients

1 ½ lemons (peeled, sliced and seeds removed)
2 apples (green preferably)
1 cucumber (peeled)
5 leaves of red lettuce
½ cup mango cubes (frozen or fresh)
2 tsp barley grass powder
16 oz. purified water

Directions

1. Blend at high speed until consistency is perfect for you – forty-five seconds usually does the trick.

Kale-Apple

This smoothie will enhance your day, give you energy and not disrupt your blood sugar.

Servings: 2

calories: 154 | sodium: 73 mg | dietary fiber: 3.2 | total fat: 1.9 g | total carbs: 21.0 g | protein: 13.7 g

Ingredients

2 cups kale or spinach
½ cup Greek yogurt
½ cup apple or orange juice
(unsweetened and de-seeded)
5 tsp flaxseeds
2 tsp maple syrup
1 cup ice cubes

Directions

1. Blend for 30 – 45 seconds or until smooth.

Zesty Lime

This is a delicious and nutritious smoothie that satisfies many people who have Type ll diabetes.

Servings: 2

calories: 484 | sodium: 59 mg | dietary fiber: 6.3 | total fat: 37.9 g | total carbs: 36.3 g | protein: 8.6 g

Ingredients

½ cup lime juice
1 cup almond milk
1 banana (frozen)
1 ½ cups kale (or spinach)
5 ice cubes
2 tbsp almond butter (or sunflower butter)
2 pitted dates

Directions

1. Blend for 30 – 45 seconds or until smooth.

Avocado

Avocados have much of what the body needs to maintain a healthy

Immune system. Avocados are full of Zinc, Selenium, Folic Acid, Iron and vitamins B6, E, A and C. If you haven't noticed yet, avocados are a true superfood.

Servings: 2

calories: 216 | sodium: 8 mg | dietary fiber: 6.3 | total fat: 11.5 g | total carbs: 30.5 g | protein: 1.9 g

Ingredients

½ avocado

½ banana

2 tbsp honey

1 cup ice cubes

½ cup spring water

1/3 cup lime juice

1 tbsp chai seeds

½ mango (peeled, pitted and cubed)

Directions

1. Blend for 30 – 45 seconds or until smooth.

Granny Green

Ginger is a natural anti-inflammatory and a strong infection fighter.

All the elements in this smoothie have a synergistic effect on your immune system. When combined, they work even more effectively to strengthen your system and keep you healthy.

Servings: 2

calories: 124 | sodium: 29 mg | dietary fiber: 4.3 | total fat: 0.5 g | total carbs: 30.8 g | protein: 1.7 g

Ingredients

1 Granny Smith apple (sliced and de-seeded)
½ pear
1 celery stalk (chopped)
1 cup kale
1 tbsp ginger
1 cup ice cubes
½ cup spring water or apple juice

Directions

1. Blend thoroughly for 30 – 45
   seconds or until smooth.

The Cold Fighter

This smoothie will not only energize you but will satisfy your hunger pangs and fight off those nasty colds in the winter.

Servings: 2

calories: 46 | sodium: 53 mg | dietary fiber: 2.1 | total fat: 0.3 g | total carbs: 10.4 g | protein: 1.5 g

Ingredients

1 carrot
½ beet (chopped)
1 celery stalk (chopped)
½ cucumber (peeled and sliced)
1 tbsp of sliced ginger
1 cup ice cubes
½ cup spring water

Directions

1. Blend until smooth – usually around 30 – 45 seconds.

Romantic Veggie

This one will have the texture of milk like you've never imagined and the tangy flavor of veggies that will be somehow familiar to you. What you will really appreciate about it though, is its ability to relax your muscles and blood pressure, giving you a youthful glow as you float several feet above the ground.

Servings: 2

calories: 55 | sodium: 51 mg | dietary fiber: 2.8 | total fat: 0.2 g | total carbs: 11.9 g | protein: 2.3 g

Ingredients

1 medium tomato

½ red bell pepper

2 cloves garlic

1 celery stalk

1 carrot (sliced)

1 cup kale (or romaine lettuce)

1 cup ice cubes

Directions

1. Blend for 30 – 45 seconds or until texture is smooth.

Royal Avocado

Silky skin is attainable with these wonderful ingredients. The avocado, in itself is a marvelous food for great skin and hair, but the synergistic effect it has when combined with the other elements is incredible.

Servings: 2

calories: 90 | sodium: 17 mg | dietary fiber: 3.1 | total fat: 0.8 g | total carbs: 21.1 g | protein: 2.3 g

Ingredients

½ avocado (ripe) or 4 tbsp almond butter

½ cucumber

1 cup kale or Bok Choy or romaine lettuce

½ banana

¾ cup blueberries

1 cup spring water or coconut water

Directions

1. We don't recommend a sweetener for this, but if you must, you must. Go lightly and use honey if necessary.

2. Blend until smooth.

Berry Burst

This most excellent smoothie wi'
burst of energy that will last for so
soy milk and flaxseeds give this berry smoothie
a stabilizing effect, so you won't feel like you're
coming down like you used to after a chocolate
bar.

Servings: 2

calories: 423 | sodium: 5 mg | dietary fiber: 11.7 |
total fat: 25.9 g | total carbs: 42.5 g | protein:
12.5g

Ingredients

> 1 cup almond or soy milk
> ½ cup blackberries
> ½ cup blueberries
> 1 banana (frozen)
> 1 tbsp honey
> 1 ½ tbsp. flaxseed
> ½ cup ice cubes

Directions

1. Blend 30 – 45 seconds or until smooth.

Green Goblin

Also, after blending, chill in refrige
blend briskly again right before ser......

This smoothie will give you energy to spare.
Your competitors will wonder how you stay so
far ahead of them all the time. Let them keep
wondering. It's good for them.

Servings: 2

calories: 133 | sodium: 32 mg | dietary fiber: 4.7 |
total fat: 0.6 g | total carbs: 33.3 g | protein: 2.3 g

Ingredients

> 1 cup kale or spinach (chopped)
> 1 apple (peeled, sliced, deseeded)
> ½ cup seedless grapes (green)
> 1 kiwi (sliced and peeled)
> 1 cup honeydew melon (shopped and peeled)

Directions

> 1. Blend for 30 – 45 seconds or until smooth.

Mean Green Machine

This one is a winner. You can drink this before or after a workout and feel great. It pumps a lot of nutrition your way and delivers protein and flavor also.

Servings: 2

calories: 62 | sodium: 26 mg | dietary fiber: 3.0 | total fat: 0.3 g | total carbs: 15.3 g | protein: 1.1 g

Ingredients

1 cup of kale or spinach (chopped)
1 stalk of celery (chopped)
1 apple (sliced)
1 tbsp lemon juice
1/3 cucumber (sliced)
1 cup ice cubes
¼ cup spring water

Directions

1. Blend until smooth – usually 30 – 45 minutes.

Apple Caramel

Sounds good, tastes even better – and it's good for you, too.

Servings: 2

calories: 313 | sodium: 225 mg | dietary fiber: 3.6 g | total fat: 1.1 g | total carbs: 77.6 g | protein: 3.9g

Ingredients

¼ cup caramel sauce
1 cup low fat vanilla yogurt
2 cups apple juice
1 tbsp cinnamon
2 tbsp sweetener (your choice)
6 ice cubes

Directions

1. Blend until texture is smooth.

Banana Cream

This low calorie dessert smoothie lives up to its name and tops it off by providing natural nutrients for energy.

Servings: 2

calories: 397 | sodium: 519 mg | dietary fiber: 3.6 g | total fat: 14.7 g | total carbs: 54.0 g | protein: 14.9 g

Ingredients

1 cup low fat vanilla yogurt
1 ½ bananas
2 cups vanilla almond milk
½ cup low fat cottage cheese
¼ cup cream cheese (low fat is okay)
½ tsp cinnamon

Directions

1. Blend for 45 seconds or until texture is smooth.

Banana Pumpkin

Banana and pumpkin are great anytime of the year and even better together – nutritionally and taste-wise.

Servings: 2

calories: 450 | sodium: 209 mg | dietary fiber: 10.3 | total fat: 17.9 g | total carbs: 63.1 g | protein: 14.3g

Ingredients

1 ½ cup soymilk or low fat milk
6 kale leaves
2 tbsp flaxseed oil
1 ½ banana
½ tsp cinnamon
1 cup pumpkin puree (canned is fine)
6 ice cubes

Directions

1. Blend until smooth – 45 seconds at high speed or until texture is smooth.

Berry Carrot

This great tasting smoothie lets you drink your way to health.

Servings: 2

calories: 420 | sodium: 251 mg | dietary fiber: 5.0 | total fat: 4.6 g | total carbs: 72.3 g | protein: 25.4 g

Ingredients

1 cup frozen berries (your choice or mixed)

1 cup low fat milk or almond milk

2 cup juice or water

1 ½ carrots

2 tbsp chia seeds

¼ cup protein powder

Directions

1. Blend at high speed for 45 seconds or until smooth.

Berry-Granate

When you mix pomegranate and berries together you get a high energy drink that's filled with antioxidants.

Servings: 2

calories: 451 | sodium: 42 mg | dietary fiber: 7.7 g | total fat: 3.0 g | total carbs: 99.4 g | protein: 7.4 g

Ingredients

2 cups silken tofu

2 cups pomegranate juice

3 cups mixed berries (fresh or frozen)

¼ cup honey or sweetener of your choice

Directions

1. Blend well until smooth – usually 45 seconds at high speed.

Cafe Banana

Add a super food to coffee and you get a wonderful wake up smoothie that will open your eyes wide.

Servings: 2

calories: 244 | sodium: 93 mg | dietary fiber: 4.4 | total fat: 3.0 g | total carbs: 39.9 g | protein: 16.3 g

Ingredients

1 ½ bananas

2 cups coffee (cold)

½ cup protein powder

½ cup low fat milk or soymilk

½ cup dry oats

Directions

1. Blend until smooth – usually 45 seconds on high speed.

Chocolate Divine

This creamy smoothie is not only divinely delicious, but it has all the elements that make it a heavenly, healthful drink.

Servings: 2

calories: 335 | sodium: 140 mg | dietary fiber: 7.7 g | total fat: 18.2 g | total carbs: 42.4 g | protein: 12.2 g

Ingredients

¼ cup cocoa powder or chocolate syrup
½ cup coconut milk
6 dates (pitted)
2 cups low fat milk or soymilk
2 tbsp sweetener (your choice)
6 ice cubes

Directions

1. Blend for 45 seconds or until smooth.

Chocolatey Date

Antioxidants and a great deal of high energy elements are provided by this great smoothie.

Servings: 2

calories: 462 | sodium: 50 mg | dietary fiber: 16.5 g | total fat: 16.2 g | total carbs: 84.7 g | protein: 14.0 g

Ingredients

1 cup pitted dates
½ cup almonds
½ cup cocoa or chocolate syrup
2 cups boiling water
1 cup silken tofu
6 ice cubes

Directions

1. Add the ice and tofu after you've let the other ingredients sit in the boiling water in the blender for ten minutes. This will soften them up for the blending phase. Blend for 45 seconds or until texture is consistently smooth.

Coconut Almond

This smoothie is high in immune protecting nutrients along with a great deal of protein and vitamin C.

Servings: 2

calories: 591 | sodium: 220 mg | dietary fiber: 8.0 | total fat: 46.7 g | total carbs: 46.4 g | protein: 6.3 g

Ingredients

1 ½ cups coconut water
1 ½ cups almond milk
2 tbsp honey or sweetener of your choice
1 cup cubed pineapple (fresh or frozen)
¼ cup shredded coconut
½ tsp vanilla extract

Directions

1. Blend for 45 seconds at high speed or until smooth.

Flaxseed Spinach

This smoothie is protein rich, has a lot of fiber and plenty of Omega-3s, all of which promote and support health.

Servings: 2

calories: 517 | sodium: 282 mg | dietary fiber: 4.9 | total fat: 26.4 g | total carbs: 57.5 g | protein: 18.4g

Ingredients

1 ½ bananas

6 strawberries (frozen or fresh)

1 tbsp flaxseed oil

¼ cup peanut butter

1 ½ cups low fat milk or soymilk

1 cup plain or vanilla low fat yogurt

Directions

1. Blend all together at high speed for 45 seconds or until smooth.

Green Tea Banana

Green tea is a great way to burn fat and stay healthy; it's also a terrific way to wake up in the morning.

Servings: 2

calories: 451 | sodium: 159 mg | dietary fiber: 7.5 g | total fat: 1.8 g | total carbs: 112.2 g | protein: 6.5 g

Ingredients

1 ½ bananas
1 honeydew melon (scooped in pieces away from rind)
1 ½ cups brewed green tea
2tbsp honey or sweetener of your choice
½ cup low fat milk or soy or almond milk

Directions

1. Blend for 45 seconds or until smooth.

KC Delight (Kale/Coconut)

When you combine a super food like Kale and a miracle food like coconut, you get a healthy concoction that is extremely delicious too.

Servings: 2

calories: 374 | sodium: 53 mg | dietary fiber: 3.4 | total fat: 14.3 g | total carbs: 62.3 g | protein: 3.1 g

Ingredients

>   1 ½ banana
>   2 cups chopped kale
>   2 tbsp flaxseed oil
>   ¼ cup honey or sweetener (your choice)
>   ½ tsp coconut extract
>   6 ice cubes

Directions

1. Blend for 45 seconds or until smooth.

Lemon Strawberry

This is not only refreshing, but it's full of energy giving vitamin C and other health supporting nutrients.

Servings: 2

calories: 168 | sodium: 136 mg | dietary fiber: 2.4 g | total fat: 5.8 g | total carbs: 19.9 g | protein: 10.2 g

Ingredients

1 cup strawberries (fresh or frozen)
2 cups low fat milk or soymilk
Ten raw almonds
¼ cup lemon juice
1 tsp lemon zest
6 ice cubes

Directions

1. Blend 45 seconds at high speed or until smooth.

Minty Spinach

Vitamin and mineral rich spinach combined with minty chocolate is hard to beat.

Servings: 2

calories: 250 | sodium: 132 mg | dietary fiber: 2.7 | total fat: 5.0 g | total carbs: 28.6 g | protein: 22.3 g

Ingredients

2 cups low fat milk or almond milk
½ cup chocolate protein powder
2 cups frozen spinach (or 3 cups fresh spinach)
½ cup dry oats
¼ tsp peppermint extract

Directions

1. Blend at high speed for 45 seconds or until smooth.

PB&J

Now you can get all the eating enjoyment of your youth plus even more nutrition and energy, by drinking it.

Servings: 2

calories: 517 | sodium: 369 mg | dietary fiber: 2.4 g | total fat: 20.0 g | total carbs: 65.7 g | protein: 21.5 g

Ingredients

¼ cup peanut butter

¼ cup jam (your choice of flavor)

6 ice cubes

½ tsp vanilla extract

2 ½ cups low fat milk or soymilk

¼ cup low fat yogurt (plain or vanilla)

Directions

1. Blend until smooth – usually 45 seconds at high speed.

Raisin Bliss

This smoothie provides long-lasting energy for a busy lifestyle.

Servings: 2

calories: 420 | sodium: 251 mg | dietary fiber: 5.0 | total fat: 4.6 g | total carbs: 72.3 g | protein: 25.4 g

Ingredients

2 bananas

½ cup protein powder (chocolate might be good here)

2 tsp cinnamon

1 cup low fat vanilla or plain yogurt

1 tbsp honey or your choice of sweetener

1 ½ cups low fat milk or soymilk

¼ cup raisins

6 ice cubes

Directions

1. Blend thoroughly at high speed for 45 seconds or until smooth.

Smoothie Sundae

Instead of ice cream, try this low calorie smoothie for energy and taste.

Servings: 2

calories: 424 | sodium: 256 mg | dietary fiber: 5.0 | total fat: 14.6 g | total carbs: 60.2 g | protein: 13.4g

Ingredients

1 cup low fat vanilla yogurt
1 ½ cups low fat chocolate milk or chocolate soymilk
1 ½ cups strawberries (fresh or frozen)
2 tsp flaxseed (ground)
½ cup chocolate or vanilla protein powder

Directions

1. Blend until smooth – usually 45 seconds at high speed.

Spunky Monkey

The three ingredients we loved as kids, chocolate, bananas and peanut butter are back for the same reasons in this smoothie: taste, (of course), they keep us full longer and they give us a lot of energy.

Servings: 2

calories: 358 | sodium: 395 mg | dietary fiber: 7.0 | total fat: 17.0 g | total carbs: 43.1 g | protein: 17.0g

Ingredients

1 ½ bananas
¼ cup peanut butter
2 cups low fat chocolate milk or chocolate soymilk
6 ice cubes
3 tbsp sweetener (your choice)

Directions

1. Blend until smooth.

Strawberry Peach

This favorite is tasty and keeps you satisfied for hours.

Servings: 2

calories: 299 | sodium: 110 mg | dietary fiber: 5.8 | total fat: 4.2 g | total carbs: 59.3 g | protein: 10.8 g

Ingredients

1 ½ bananas
1 ½ cup strawberries (frozen or fresh)
2 cups low fat milk or soymilk
¼ cup chia seeds
2 tbsp honey (or your choice of sweetener)

Directions

1. Blend thoroughly at high speed for 45 seconds or until smooth.

Veggie Spice

This smoothie has bite and nutrition, along with providing an ample source of high energy.

Servings: 2

calories: 252 | sodium: 170 mg | dietary fiber: 10.4 | total fat: 14.7 g | total carbs: 29.4 g | protein: 3.6g

Ingredients

1 cup avocado
¼ cup lemon juice
14 oz. carrot juice
Dash of cayenne pepper
1 ½ tbsp. fresh ginger (grated)
6 ice cubes

Directions

1. Blend for 45 seconds at high speed or until smooth.

Waterberry

Combine watermelon with st
you get this wonderful mixt
nutrition and energy.

Servings: 2

calories: 219 | sodium: 195 mg | dietary fiber: 1.7 |
total fat: 3.2 g | total carbs: 25.8 g | protein: 20.3 g

Ingredients

½ cup low fat milk or soymilk
Medium-sized seedless watermelon
(scooped out in cubes from rind)
1 cup strawberries (frozen or fresh)
1 cup low fat yogurt
¼ cup protein powder
6 ice cubes

Directions

1. Blend for 45 seconds at high speed
   or until smooth.

Flaxseed Supreme

Flaxseeds provide Omega-3, which is a good fatty acid and is beneficial to optimal heart function. Antioxidants, along with minerals and vitamins from the other ingredients, strengthen the body, including the heart, against infections and failure.

Servings: 2

calories: 240 | sodium: 26 mg | dietary fiber: 8.9 | total fat: 11.3 g | total carbs: 33.7 g | protein: 4.4 g

Ingredients

>   1 banana
>   ½ orange (sliced0
>   ½ cup berries (your choice)
>   ½ avocado
>   1 ½ cups kale or romaine lettuce
>   1 tbsp flaxseeds (ground)
>   1 cup spring water

Directions

1. Blend ingredients together for 30 – 45 seconds or until smooth.

Hardy Heart

This smoothie is full of fiber, which can remove toxins from your intestines and lower your cholesterol. The greens in this tasty treat are also good for maintaining a healthy heart rate.

Servings: 2

calories: 130 | sodium: 77 mg | dietary fiber: 17.8 | total fat: 0.5 g | total carbs: 38.2 g | protein: 2.3 g

Ingredients

    1 cup cucumber (peeled and sliced)
    1 cup kale or spinach
    1 celery stalk (chopped)
    ½ cup parsley (chopped)
    1 tbsp psyllium husks (or Metamucil)
    1 apple (peeled and de-seeded)
    2 tbsp lemon juice
    1 tbsp lime juice

Directions

    1. Blend for 30 – 45 seconds or until smooth.

Pomegranate Pump

This is full of antioxidants and will get your circulation stimulated and your blood pumping in the right direction. It can also help unclog your arteries.

Servings: 2

calories: 200 | sodium: 93 mg | dietary fiber: 1.5 | total fat: 1.7 g | total carbs: 36.6 g | protein: 7.5 g

Ingredients

½ banana

6 strawberries

1 cup plain yogurt

1 cup pomegranate juice

½ cup ice cubes

Directions

1. Blend until smooth – usually 30 – 45 seconds.

Good Mood Oatmeal

Oatmeal tends to level out blood sugar levels and it has a lot of fiber too, which helps eliminate toxins in the intestines. Walnuts are chock full of Omega-3 which works on your brain cells and lifts your mood.

Servings: 2

calories: 295 | sodium: 118 mg | dietary fiber: 4.6 | total fat: 14.9 g | total carbs: 24.8 g | protein: 15.5g

Ingredients

¼ cup rolled oats
1 cup plain yogurt
½ cup blackberries or blueberries
¼ cup walnuts (chopped)
1 tbsp walnut oil
½ cup soy milk
½ cup spring water

Directions

1. Blend for 30 – 45 seconds or until smooth.

Happy Green

Some people have told us that this smoothie changed their mood from dark to light within minutes. Of course, we are not suggesting that this is a clinical study, but eating certain nutrients has been shown to alter moods simply because of what the vitamins and minerals and other elements can do to the brain function.

Flaxseed, for example, has been shown to help many depressed people when taken on a regular basis. Are we going to argue with that? Absolutely not.

Servings: 2

calories: 528 | sodium: 76 mg | dietary fiber: 6.1 | total fat: 30.0 g | total carbs: 57.3 g | protein: 15.9g

Ingredients

1 cup kale or spinach
¼ cup Greek yogurt
1 cup soy or almond milk
1 tbsp flaxseed (ground)
3 tbsp honey
1 banana (frozen if possible)
¼ cup blueberries or blackberries

½ cup ice cubes

Directions

1. Blend for 30 – 45 seconds or until smooth.

Up, Up And Away

This is a great mood enhancer. Swiss chard has a lot of magnesium, which can increase energy levels and put us in a good mood.

Servings: 2

calories: 80 | sodium: 41 mg | dietary fiber: 2.8 | total fat: 0.4 g | total carbs: 20.0 g | protein: 1.3 g

Ingredients

1 banana
1 tsp ginger (sliced)
1 cup Swiss chard
½ cup blueberries
1 cup spring water or coconut water
½ cup ice

Directions

1. Blend for 30 – 45 seconds or until smooth.

Oatmeal

We all know why Mom cooked oatmeal for breakfast. Because she loved us, is the right answer. The second right answer is because it was nourishing and kept us full for hours. Same here, only we've added strawberries and bananas and milk for extra protein, antioxidants and potassium. This will keep any athlete going for several hours.

Servings: 2

calories: 203 | sodium: 60 mg | dietary fiber: 4.3 | total fat: 4.1 g | total carbs: 36.1 g | protein: 7.6 g

Ingredients

½ cup rolled oats
1 cup milk (soy or almond is okay too)
1 banana
½ cup strawberries

Directions

1. Only add sweetener if needed.

2. Blend for 30 – 45 seconds or until smooth.

Peanut Butter - Banana

This athletic smoothie will stick to your ribs while giving you plenty of protein and electrolytes for endurance.

Servings: 2

calories: 315 | sodium: 184 mg | dietary fiber: 4.0 | total fat: 20.2 g | total carbs: 23.8 g | protein: 15.8g

Ingredients

½ cup tofu
½ cup milk (almond, rice or soy milk is ok)
4 tbsp peanut butter
1 banana (frozen)

Directions

1. If sweetener is desired, we recommend honey or blackstrap molasses – to taste.

2. Blend until smooth – 30 – 45 seconds.

Banana-Berry

This is a simple smoothie but highly effective when it comes to dealing with stress. The potassium, magnesium and zinc from the peanut butter and banana, plus all the vitamin C and antioxidants from the berries are going to feel like the stress is just flying away.

Servings: 2

calories: 368 | sodium: 77 mg | dietary fiber: 6.7 | total fat: 20.2 g | total carbs: 43.3 g | protein: 10.0g

Ingredients

1 banana (frozen if possible)
½ cup berries (your choice)
½ cup ice cubes
½ cup almond or soy milk
2 tbsp honey
2 tbsp peanut butter

Directions

1. Blend for 30 – 45 seconds or until smooth.

Grapefruit- Kale

Stress be gone...That's what this smoothie is really saying. The potassium, magnesium, iron and vitamins A, C, B6 and D in the bananas alone are powerful stress relievers. But when working together with grapefruit, kale and coconut oil, you can add even more vitamins and some hard working minerals to combat any stress in your life.

Servings: 2

calories: 260 | sodium: 18 mg | dietary fiber: 2.4 | total fat: 13.8 g | total carbs: 36.9 g | protein: 1.9 g

Ingredients

½ grapefruit (peeled, chopped and pitted)
1 banana
2 tbsp honey
1 cup kale or spinach or romaine lettuce
½ cup ice cubes
2 tbsp coconut oil
1 cup spring water

Directions

1. Blend until smooth – usually 30 – 45 seconds.

Mint-Fennel-Pineapple

Besides all the vitamins and minerals in the other ingredients, avocados bring the B vitamins and potassium which help lower blood pressure. Fennel is a great substance that aids in digestion and it also helps calm you down.

Servings: 2

calories: 133 | sodium: 19 mg | dietary fiber: 5.1 | total fat: 9.9 g | total carbs: 11.9 g | protein: 1.7 g

Ingredients

½ oz fresh mint (chopped)

½ avocado (sliced)

½ cup fennel (chopped)

½ cup pineapple (crushed from can is ok or fresh sliced)

1 cup spring water

½ cup ice cubes

Directions

1. Blend together until smooth – usually 30 – 45 seconds.

Apple Pie

Just as filling and just like apple pie, only without the crust. It will keep you feeling full and like you just had dessert instead of a wholesome healthy smoothie.

Servings: 2

calories: 520 | sodium: 251 mg | dietary fiber: 6.9 | total fat: 11.6 g | total carbs: 93.6 g | protein: 16.1g

Ingredients

> 12 oz. plain or vanilla low fat yogurt
> 1 cup of low fat milk or soymilk
> 2 tsp apple pie spice
> 2 sliced apples (use your favorite kind)
> 4 tbsp almond or cashew butter
> 8 ice cubes

Directions

1. Blend all together at high speed for about 45 seconds or until texture is smooth.

Avocado Fiesta

This refreshing fusion of citrus and avocado will fill you up and energize you. It also enhances and supports your immune system and fights off infections.

Servings: 2

calories: 137 | sodium: 3 mg | dietary fiber: 4.8 | total fat: 0.7 g | total carbs: 34.9 g | protein: 2.0 g

Ingredients

1 ½ cups orange juice
1 ½ cups strawberry or raspberry juice
2 peeled and very ripe avocados
¾ cup frozen strawberries or raspberries
2 tbsp sweetener of your choice

Directions

1. Blend for 45 seconds at high speed or until texture is smooth.

Avocado - Swiss Chard

This is like drinking your salad and getting even more of a feeling of fullness that keeps your appetite satisfied. The avocado is at work again. It has so many nutrients that are good for you, plus it helps keep you full for hours at a time. It has Selenium, Zinc, Iron and plenty of B vitamins, along with vitamins A, C and E.

You're also going to get a lot of fiber from the flaxseeds and the avocado, which will flush out toxins and keep your lower abdomen feeling less bloated.

Servings: 2

calories: 219 | sodium: 83 mg | dietary fiber: 7.4 | total fat: 12.4 g | total carbs: 24.6 g | protein: 5.1 g

Ingredients

> 1 cup Swiss chard (chopped)
> ½ avocado (sliced)
> 1 banana
> 2 tbsp lemon juice
> ¼ cup fresh mint (chopped)
> 1 tbsp flaxseeds (ground)
> ½ cup soy milk
> ½ cup ice cubes

1 cup spring water

Directions

1. Blend for 30 – 45 seconds or until smooth.

Banana - Choco Split

This one tastes like a treat and is full of protein and nutrients and still remains low in calories. It also will give you that full feeling that will help you not to want to snack.

Servings: 2

calories: 246 | sodium: 95 mg | dietary fiber: 8.1 | total fat: 7.4 g | total carbs: 40.4 g | protein: 16.8 g

Ingredients

¼ cup cocoa powder (or chocolate syrup)
1 ½ bananas
¾ cup tofu
1 ½ cups low fat milk or soy milk
3 tbsp sweetener (your choice)

Directions

1. Blend all until smooth – about 45 seconds at high speed.

Banana/Peanut Butter Delight

This is a great low calorie meal replacer, full of vitamins, minerals and protein. It will remind you of your youth and give you the same amount of energy you had back then.

Servings: 2

calories: 742 | sodium: 166 mg | dietary fiber: 6.7 | total fat: 46.9 g | total carbs: 41.6 g | protein: 49.5g

Ingredients

1 banana
1 ¼ cup low fat milk (or soy milk)
2/3 cup smooth peanut butter (low fat preferably)
2 tbsp protein powder
8 ice cubes

Directions

1. Blend on high speed until texture is smooth.

Berry Berry Yummy

The mixed berries in this smoothie provide antioxidants and the yogurt and protein powder give you staying power with much needed protein.

Servings: 2

calories: 229 | sodium: 100 mg | dietary fiber: 5.1 | total fat: 2.0 g | total carbs: 49.2 g | protein: 5.6 g

Ingredients

1 ½ cups frozen mixed berries
½ banana
6 ice cubes
1 ½ cups plain or vanilla low fat yogurt (or milk, low fat)
1 tbsp sweetener (your choice)

Directions

1. Blend on high speed for 45 seconds or until texture is smooth.

Blue Smoothie

Blueberries contain natural antioxidants, plenty of vitamins and necessary minerals such as iron, manganese, calcium and copper. The recipe below serves two and is a delicious, low calorie drink that will keep you feeling full.

Servings: 2

calories: 222 | sodium: 71 mg | dietary fiber: 3.2 | total fat: 0.0 g | total carbs: 34.6 g | protein: 3.7 g

Ingredients

2/3 cup soy protein

1 large banana

½ cup frozen blueberries

1 tbsp flaxseed oil

16 oz. water

1 tbsp honey or sweetener of your choice

6 ice cubes (if desired)

Directions

1. Blend for about 45 seconds or until texture is smooth.

Cashew Banana

Perfect for weight loss and to keep you full.

Servings: 2

calories: 350 | sodium: 64 mg | dietary fiber: 4.4 |
total fat: 16.5 g | total carbs: 44.3 g | protein: 9.1 g

Ingredients

2 tbsp cashew butter

1 ½ banana

1 tbsp flaxseed oil

1 cup low fat yogurt (plain or vanilla)

3 tbsp sweetener (your choice)

1 tbsp vanilla extract.

Directions

1. Blend until smooth, usually around 45 seconds at high speed.

Citrus Joy

Tangy and sweet, this smoothie will satisfy your hunger and keep you going for hours.

Servings: 2

calories: 393 | sodium: 207 mg | dietary fiber: 5.5 | total fat: 13.9 g | total carbs: 52.2 g | protein: 12.7g

Ingredients

> 12 oz. citrus flavored yogurt (your choice0
> 2 oranges cut into pieces
> 1½ cups soymilk or low fat milk
> 1½ tbsp. flaxseed oil
> 8 ice cubes

Directions

1. Blend ingredients for 45 seconds at high speed or until consistency is smooth.

Grab Bag

You pick the fruit you have on hand and add a few other tidbits and you're ready to go. The fruits below can be substituted with any you prefer or have on hand at home.

Servings: 2

calories: 782 | sodium: 502 mg | dietary fiber: 11.8 | total fat: 17.5 g | total carbs: 126.2 g | protein: 34.1 g

Ingredients

1 banana
½ cup apple slices
1 ½ oranges (peeled and sectioned)
3 tbsp honey (or your choice of sweetener)
8 ice cubes.1 cup low fat milk or soymilk

Directions

1. At high speed, blend for 45 seconds or until texture is smooth.

Hawaiian Supreme

This low calorie, high fiber smoothie is a perfect way to feel full and avoid snacks. The right way to lose weight and keep it off.

Servings: 2

calories: 263 | sodium: 110 mg | dietary fiber: 3.3 | total fat: 15.9 g | total carbs: 27.5 g | protein: 6.8 g

Ingredients

8 oz. pineapple chunks with juice (canned is fine)
1½ cups low fat milk or soymilk
2 tbsp flaxseed oil
8 ice cubes
3 tbsp sweetener (your choice)

Directions

1. Blend until texture is smooth – about 45 seconds at high speed.

Hot Tomato, Hot Tomato ...

This is a Bloody Mary without the alcohol and side effects. You only get energized with a natural dose of vitamins and minerals with this delicious smoothie.

Servings: 2

calories: 95 | sodium: 462 mg | dietary fiber: 3.6 | total fat: 0.5 g | total carbs: 22.3 g | protein: 2.7 g

Ingredients

½ cup apple juice
1 cup tomato juice
1 ½ cups chopped tomatoes
2/3 cup chopped carrots
2/3 cup chopped celery
2/3 tsp hot sauce
9 ice cubes

Directions

1. Blend until smooth – about 45 seconds at high speed.

Kale-Ginger

Kale is one of the most nutritious leafy greens out there and it has an abundance of vitamins C and K and betacarotene, along with antioxidants and anti-inflammatory benefits. Kale is also a good detoxifier, which just means it helps the body rid itself of toxins. That in itself is a good weight loss benefit, but coupled with its cancer fighting abilities and Kale is truly a superfood.

Ginger is often compared to caffeine as a weight loss aid. It certainly aids in digestion and gastrointestinal problems but now many people are adding it to their weight loss regimens with great success.

Servings: 1

calories: 187 | sodium: 82 mg | dietary fiber: 8.9 | total fat: 1.2 g | total carbs: 44.4 g | protein: 5.7 g

Ingredients

1 cup kale or spinach or romaine lettuce
1 apple (peeled, sliced and de-seeded)
¼ bunch parsley
½ cucumber (peeled and sliced)
1 celery stalk (chopped)

½ lemon (peeled, sliced and de-seeded)
2 tsp ginger (chopped)
1 cup spring water

Directions

1. Blend until smooth – usually 30 – 45 seconds.

Key Lime

Tangy, delicious, low calorie and full of Vitamin C.

Servings: 2

calories: 2,939 | sodium: 499 mg | dietary fiber: 1.9 | total fat: 127.8 g | total carbs: 420.6 g | protein: 37.7 g

Ingredients

¾ cup sliced and peeled lime
1 ½ cup low fat milk or soy milk
1 12 cups lime sherbet
2/3 cup strawberries
8 ice cubes.

Directions

1. Blend on high speed for 45 seconds or until texture is smooth.

Mango Bliss

Mangos are tasty, sweet and full of vitamins C, A, B6, along with natural fiber to keep you feeling full and reduce the risk of colon cancer.

Servings: 2

calories: 207 | sodium: 73 mg | dietary fiber: 5.5 | total fat: 7.8 g | total carbs: 37.5 g | protein: 2.7 g

Ingredients

>1 cup mango juice (bottled is fine)
>2 tbsp sweetener (your choice)
>2 tbsp lime or lemon juice
>5 ice cubes
>½ cup mashed ripe avocado
>½ cup plain or vanilla low fat yogurt
>½ cup mangoes – cubed

Directions

1. Blend ingredients at high speed until texture is smooth as you desire.

Melon Perfection

This smoothie is extremely low calorie with hours of staying power.

Servings: 2

calories: 129 | sodium: 69 mg | dietary fiber: 7.8 | total fat: 0.7 g | total carbs: 30.3 g | protein: 2.8 g

Ingredients

3 cups cantaloupe pieces
1 ½ cups raspberries or strawberries (frozen or fresh)
8 ice cubes
1 ½ cups chopped lettuce leaves (Romaine preferably, or to taste)

Directions

1. Blend until smooth – about 45 seconds at high speed.

Mocha Espresso Wake Up

This low calorie, high-energy smoothie will wake you up and make you full for hours. There is a lot of natural occurring antioxidants, protein and even caffeine for your morning get up and go.

Servings: 2

calories: 256 | sodium: 108 mg | dietary fiber: 12.7 | total fat: 11.6 g | total carbs: 24.4 g | protein: 13.9g

Ingredients

4 teaspoons cocoa powder

2 shots espresso

1 cup low-fat plain or vanilla yogurt

2 tbsp chia seeds

2 tbsp sweetener (Your choice)

6 ice cubes

Directions

1. Blend ingredients for about 45 seconds on high speed or until consistency is smooth and even throughout.

154

Peachy Keeno

Peaches are quite refreshing when they're in season, and they provide plenty of energy. The chia seeds give you a full feeling that lasts for hours.

Servings: 2

calories: 195 | sodium: 112 mg | dietary fiber: 8.9 | total fat: 5.1 g | total carbs: 29.9 g | protein: 10.3 g

Ingredients

1 ½ cups sliced frozen or fresh peaches
1 tbsp chia seeds
1 ½ cups low fat or non-fat milk
4 ice cubes
3 tbsp sweetener (your choice)

Directions

1. Blend on high speed for 45 seconds or until texture is smooth.

Raspberry Treat

Raspberries are rich in minerals such as potassium, copper, iron, manganese and magnesium and high in vitamins K and B-complex. These vitamins are extremely helpful in aiding our metabolism, which in turn is responsible for weight-loss. The dark chocolate in the recipe adds antioxidants, which increases blood flow.

Servings: 2

calories: 557 | sodium: 223 mg | dietary fiber: 6.7 | total fat: 13.2 g | total carbs: 102.2 g | protein: 14.6g

Ingredients

10 oz. plain or vanilla low fat yogurt
1 cup low fat, skim milk or soymilk
½ cup dark chocolate chips
1 ½ cups raspberries (frozen or fresh)
1 ½ cup raspberry juice
6 ice cubes

Directions

1. Blend these ingredients together for 45 seconds at high speed and then drink away.

Red Banana

ias fill you up while providing essential ...ents such as magnesium, potassium, copper and vitamin B6, which are great bones, heart and blood pressure.

Servings: 2

calories: 272 | sodium: 110 mg | dietary fiber: 6.8 | total fat: 2.4 g | total carbs: 54.4 g | protein: 9.9 g

Ingredients

6 ice cubes

½ cup apple, orange or juice of your choice

1 ½ bananas

1 ½ cup strawberries

1 sliced orange

1 cup low fat plain or vanilla yogurt

Directions

1. Enjoy this terrific drink after you blend ingredients at high speed for 45 seconds or until texture is smooth throughout.

Strawberry/Spinach

This low calorie smoothie is loaded with protein, vitamins, minerals and lots of flavor.

Servings: 2

calories: 206 | sodium: 156 mg | dietary fiber: 2.2 | total fat: 4.6 g | total carbs: 23.8 g | protein: 16.5 g

Ingredients

½ banana

¼ cup orange juice

¼ cup strawberries (frozen or fresh)

6 oz. plain or vanilla yogurt

½ cup spinach

4 baby carrots

¼ cup protein powder

1 tsp flaxseed oil

4 ice cubes

1 tbsp dry oatmeal

Directions

1. Blend together for 45 seconds at high speed or until smooth.

Tooty-Fruity

This one's all about low calorie great taste, energy and meal replacement.

Servings: 2

calories: 463 | sodium: 388 mg | dietary fiber: 3.8 | total fat: 7.4 g | total carbs: 63.7 g | protein: 34.6 g

Ingredients

2 frozen bananas
1 ½ cups peach slices (frozen or fresh)
½ cup blueberries (or strawberries)
1 cup low fat plain or vanilla yogurt
2 tbsp protein powder
½ cup low fat milk or soymilk

Directions

1. Blend for 45 seconds at high speed.

Ice Cream-Less

This smoothie tastes wonderful without the ice cream of the previous smoothie, proving that eating healthy can be a tasty endeavor. It can also be a healthy one tow. Plenty of vitamins and minerals and protein for those growing bodies and minds.

Servings: 2

calories: 165 | sodium: 67 mg | dietary fiber: 3.4 | total fat: 2.5 g | total carbs: 32.0 g | protein: 4.8 g

Ingredients

> 1 mango (pitted and sliced)
> 1 cup soy milk
> ½ cup ice cubes
> ½ banana

Directions

> 1. Blend for 30 – 45 seconds or until smooth.

Peanut Butter Madness

Yes, it does say ice cream in this recipe. We've found that kids, like everyone else, have to want to change their eating habits. So, we felt that ice cream in the first smoothie would break the ice, so to speak, and let them know that eating healthy isn't always a tasteless routine. Anyway, try this out and maybe substitute the ice cream with a frozen soy dessert, which may have the same, desired effect.

Servings: 2

calories: 333 | sodium: 94 mg | dietary fiber: 2.2 | total fat: 22.5 g | total carbs: 20.5 g | protein: 15.3g

Ingredients

½ cup vanilla ice cream
¼ cup natural peanut butter
1 cup milk (soy or almond milk is ok)
½ cup ice cubes

Directions

1. Blend together until smooth – usually 30 – 45 seconds.

The Hybrid

You can fool your kids with this one. They'll never know that there are leafy greens in this smoothie. It will look and taste like a berry delight from the very first. Plenty of vitamin C and antioxidants, along with protein to keep your little treasure happy and healthy.

Servings: 2

calories: 77 | sodium: 16 mg | dietary fiber: 2.2 | total fat: 0.4 g | total carbs: 18.0 g | protein: 1.9 g

Ingredients

½ cup spring water
½ cup orange juice
½ cup strawberries
½ cup blueberries
1 cup kale or spinach (chopped)

Directions

1. Blend until smooth – usually 30 – 45 seconds.

Bonus

Smoothie Ingredients Shopping List

Isn't it exciting when you decide to make something in the kitchen on the spur of the moment and you actually have the ingredients in your pantry? Even though to some of us, having a well-stocked pantry sounds like an everyday occurrence, to a lot of us it sounds like a dream or a fairy tale because almost every time we want to whip something up in the kitchen, we're missing a few of the key ingredients. We simply didn't think ahead to when we might want to make a smoothie, and the recipe in our minds and taste buds called for yogurt, Goji berries or even something as common as an apple.

Somehow we just didn't prepare for that unexpected situation.

Here is a list of smoothie ingredients that a lot of us would like to always have on hand for those unanticipated moments of appetite inspirations.

LIQUIDS, Etc.

- Apple juice or your preference
- Soymilk
- Low fat milk
- Almond milk
- Purified water
- Yogurt

Fruits

- Bananas – One of the most common ingredients in the smoothie world.
- Apples – Vitamin A, C, D, iron, Calcium and magnesium.
- Blueberries – Flavorful and chock-full of antioxidants.

- Mangos – Vitamin C, A, B6, GABA and lots of fiber.
- Papaya – Vitamin C, D, B6 and A, along with iron, magnesium and calcium.
- Raspberries – Antioxidant and anti-inflammatory.
- Pineapple – Vitamin C, A and B complex, along with manganese and copper.
- Strawberries – Vitamin C and plenty of minerals.
- Oranges – Vitamin C and fiber.
- Kiwi – Loaded with Vitamin C.
- Dates – Sweet and full of amino acids and fiber.
- Pears – Antioxidant.
- Goji berries – Aids in well-being, quality of sleep and weight control.

Greens

These greens are considered Superfoods, along with many of the fruits listed above.

Superfoods are simply 'Exceptional" foods that have exceptional nutritional properties, which are thought to be highly beneficial our to health.

- Kale – Has Vitamin C and A and some important flavonoids.
- Spinach – Vitamin K, C, Beta-carotene, iron, magnesium, calcium and protein.
- Swiss Chard – Vitamin E and C and is an antioxidant.
- Dandelion greens – Vitamin C, B6, potassium, calcium and iron.
- Cilantro – Tasty and is a detoxifier.
- Bok Choy – Vitamin A, C, K, magnesium, potassium, manganese, calcium and iron.
- Mint leaves – refreshing and antioxidant.

NUTS And SEEDS And OTHER ESSENTIALS

- Almonds – full of protein and fiber.
- Cashews – Low fat and high in minerals.
- Walnuts – Vitamin E, flavonoids and is good for the heart.

- Chia seeds – Low calorie, high in fiber, protein and minerals.

- Flaxseeds – Antioxidant and high in fiber.

- Omega-3 fish oil – Anti-inflammatory and helps fight heart disease.

Powders And Sweeteners

- Protein powder – Soy based, whey or vegan based – your choice.

- Honey is preferable from a natural and healthy stand point.

About The Author

Lisa Brian is a San Francisco Bay Area-based health writer and chef who has been blending superfood smoothies since she was a little girl.

Living an active lifestyle in health-oriented Marin, she's always on the lookout for new and exciting foods to put into her blender. If they maximize nutrition and tastiness, she'll try the new recipe on some friends, and eventually publish the recipes which make it through her various popularity tests.

Check out her upcoming blog on superfood smoothies and Ninja Blender tech (soon to be announced :).

Made in the USA
Middletown, DE
15 February 2017